Nalisa's UNIVERSE

A Collection of Poems

NALISA CHOPRA

Om Books International

First published in 2024 by

Om Books International

Corporate & Editorial Office
A-12, Sector 64, Noida 201 301
Uttar Pradesh, India
Phone: +91 120 477 4100
Email: editorial@ombooks.com
Website: www.ombooksinternational.com

Sales Office
107, Ansari Road, Darya Ganj,
New Delhi 110 002, India
Phone: +91 11 4000 9000
Email: sales@ombooks.com
Website: www.ombooks.com

ISBN: 978-93-5376-963-5

Printed in India

10 9 8 7 6 5 4 3 2 1

NALISA'S UNIVERSE

Foreword By

Mrs. Vinita Dawra Nangia

Poetry has the power to bring about fundamental changes in minds and hearts. A poem emanates from deep within a poet and speaks to the soul of the reader. All fetters fall, and the soul breaks free with the power of a good poem.

"Everything has beauty, but not everyone sees it," said Confucius. And so, it falls to the lot of those sensitive souls amidst us who do see that beauty, admire, and internalize it, to then share their perspective with the world. Such sensitive souls are the poets amongst us. They are the ones who shine light on what often goes unnoticed and unappreciated in the actual world. With the power of metaphor and imagery, good poems stir our very being and call for change.

Poetry has never been, and is unlikely to ever become, a popular pursuit. It has always been the retreat of deep-thinking, soulful people who prefer to connect with themselves and others at a deeper level. It is an outpouring of raw emotions sculpted into beautiful words and verse, the reading of which has the strength to ignite souls with messages that may heal, incite, hurt, thrill, sadden, surprise, please, irritate, or send into deep reflection. What could be more powerful!

We live in a world that lacks poetry and romance, as it does the finer emotions of life. In a world dominated by social media, poetic voices are easily smothered, along with all other better aspects of life. The good and honest often retreats, as the ugly and fake takes forefront in a battle of sparring, criticism, bitterness, cynicism and the cancel culture.

In such a scenario, a young poet's voice is always welcome. For, it signals hope that a section of youth is still looking beyond the surface to try and understand the world through their emotions, to bring a new perspective to life and its goings on. And when this fresh look at the world is constructed into beautiful, meaningful words, that becomes the catalyst that the world needs to be able to introspect and begin the process of change. And this is what the poet's job is – to lift the veil and start off a process of questions and doubts, subtly point a path and get the process started. Giving solutions is not poetry; just stirring the cauldron is more like it. It is rightly said, a poem is never finished; it can only be abandoned.

However powerful or stirring a poem is, it always starts from a place of tranquillity – it is an outpouring of emotions. As Wordsworth famously said, "Poetry is the spontaneous overflow of powerful feelings: it takes its origin from emotion recollected in tranquillity."

Nalisa Chopra's poems too begin from a space of tranquillity, from emotions collected in quietude – surprising in one so young! From a scene at a railway station to thoughts gathered while lying in a hammock; from sighting a mystical entity in the woods to books kept in shelves, or stories that a pair of eyes tell – the young poet shows keen observation and a maturity beyond her years. Her verses reflect the curious world of a teenager who finds Sita in Ramayana as inspiring as the whirlwind romance of *The Great Gatsby*. In her poems she touches upon tiny nuances of love as well as idyllic moments that mark her life full of dreams, ambitions, infatuations and a rock-solid family bond.

Particularly touching for me is "Braided My Hair" –

The one who braided my hair,
Ran her fingers through them like silk strands,
The scent of mustard oil,
The grease from churned butter in her hands.

....

She went slow...so she could complete a tale of faraway fantasy,
The one that left her scent, in my braided hair for me.

Adding a magical touch to the poems are the illustrations that reflect the imagery that emanates from Nalisa's mind.

This collection of poems deserves a sit-down in your comfort zone on a beautiful, tranquil eve, when you are ready to delve into your inner world and allow a young poet to unveil the beauty that surrounds you – a beauty in everything, everywhere – which is unseen by us most of the time!

VINITA DAWRA NANGIA
SEPT 2022
Executive editor, The Times of India; Festival director, Times Literature Festival; Founder, Write India

***

Testimony By

Mrs. ANSHU KHANNA

"Don't limit a girl to your own learning.
For she was born in another time."
- RABINDRANATH TAGORE

Whenever I meet Nalisa, I am reminded of Guru Rabindranath's deep views on unfettered upbringing. Nalisa Chopra, young poet, a true prodigy and a wordsmith in the making, is a product of a much-loved household, where every child is given her own arena to excel; her parents walking the extra hundred miles to ensure her dreams are met and hopes fulfilled.

What do you say to a girl like Nalisa? Dressed like any of her teen-age contemporaries. As fond of going out, meeting friends, nursing infatuations and following fads. Yet scrape the surface and what you have is a river of thoughts that run deep. So, so deep that it is almost uncanny.

Listening to her poems across a computer in the thick of Covid times I was so awe struck with her perceptions of love, life and belonging. How she could turn everyday moments into points to ponder. How she so delicately expresses her feminism through the veil of words that rhyme. How she was so simply succulent with her thoughts.

That she will go far, I have no doubt. I can almost see her walking through the portals of an Ivy league college, enroute to the library, a set of books in one hand and an uber luxury bag in the other. All I hope is that in the cacophony of everyday life she should never forget the cadence of stringing two whimsical lines together and saying it all, simply so.

Thank you for making me part of the project and God bless.

Mrs. Anshu Khanna
Founder, Royal Fables Private Limited and
Goodword Media Services Pvt Ltd

***

CONTENT

01 CHAPTER MYSTICAL

02 CHAPTER STORYTELLING

03 CHAPTER NATURE

04 CHAPTER MEMORIES

05 CHAPTER ROMANCE

06 CHAPTER FEMINIST

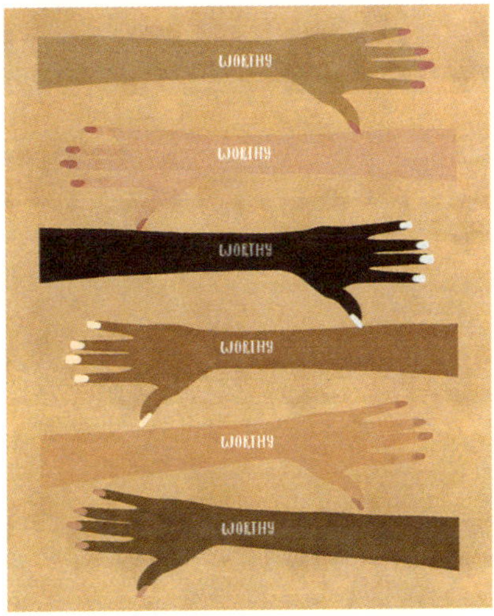

07 CHAPTER ME

01
CHAPTER

Mystical

1.

Tomorrow Land

Somewhere in tomorrow land,
There is a brown sea and blue sand.
Glitter and sparkle fall off the trees,
Stars keep floating with the cool breeze.
Elysian mountains made of gold,
And magical stories being told.

Pretty astounding? I know it might be sounding,
But true it is for the people of this land;
The ones that swim in the brown sea,
And walk on the blue sand.

2.

My Beauty

When I look in the mirror, I love what I see,
The beautiful way God has created me.
The way my hair falls over my neck,
And my gorgeous deep brown eyes,
Reflecting those long black waves, the depth
of the ocean and the skies.

My skin soft as a pillow and as white as snow,
The smile on my face wearing a natural glow.
My beautiful body, which I love to see,
The beautiful way God has created me.

3.

A Living from a Memory

Make a living from a memory, not one but
Many where you had a blast;
If you want to live, then live as such,
You would want to remember and cherish the past.

It can never be too much of what we call fun,
Not want to keep it or desire it, never will you find one.
Go and dance outside in the rain, dance outside
on a rainy evening,
Snatch the karaoke from your friend, pour your
heart out and sing.

Go and buy that dress you want, the one you
have been admiring for days;
It has become tired of resting in the store,
Now wants to come home, it says.
Buy a cake from the bakery and give a child a half,
Run around the streets with joy
and make a stranger laugh.

Call up your crush and tell them,
tell them what you feel;
Take something from your sibling's wardrobe
Without telling them of the steal.
Leave a present at the neighbour's doorstep
And let them wonder it's whose;

But pick something they would like,
Something they would choose.

Go and catch that train now...
The train for which you don't have the ticket you need,
Without knowing where you will end up,
Which town or country would the train lead?
Don't worry about the aftermath,
Life is too short to do so
Just enjoy and live in the moment...
for life is like a moving train, you know.
Don't wonder where you'll end up,
Don't keep thinking when and how,
Do something fun and forget everything else,
for you can say you have done it now.

Laugh a little, love a little,
forget for a while all the sorrow;
Live as if it's your only chance...
live as if there's no tomorrow!
To make a living from a memory not one but many where
You had a blast, if you want to live then live as such
You would want to remember and cherish the past!

4.

An Unknown Road

I head down an unknown road,
Without knowing if the diesel is enough or low,
Without knowing if I'll reach before dark,
For I don't know how far I will go.
Without knowing the weather ahead,
For will it rain or become cold?

Without knowing if the tyres can push,
Through the snow, or pulling through pools
Of water the engine can hold;
Without knowing how much I need to race her,
Or how much battery is present in my phone;
For I might need to make an important call,
In case I'd get left behind alone.
Without knowing if she will be comfortable,
And withstand any hurdles on the road,
For I always drove her in the routes she loved,
Never in the adventurous mode.

Without knowing if she will get tired,
And come to a halt during the day.
Without knowing if I have an extra tyre,
Or if there is a fuel pump on the way.
Without knowing if I will get my sweet, evening
Cardamom tea even at a small tea stall.
Without knowing if I will get a route with
No traffic or signal enough to make a call.

Without knowing if I have enough food
In the car or if there is an eatery en route;
Without knowing where it will lead me today,
My spontaneous youth.
Without knowing if I need to worry, for it may
Diverge into a route I know,
Without knowing if I'll reach today, for I
Don't know how far I will go.

5.

Goddess Sita I Stan

Goddess Sita I stan, for she was a woman
with the will power of a man.
She truly loved and kept her words, kept her
words to him each while
She left the comfort of her palace to stay
with him during exile,
She remained loyal to her subjects, so true
was her love to loyalty,
But could another princess do so, belonging
to rich royalty?

When I read about her graceful story, I was
mesmerised and relieved,
For she was a woman who knew the power of love,
She was a woman who believed.
She heartfully believed in the power of love, of when
When she was trapped in that treasury,
From which only the touch of Lord Ram, the touch of Lord
Ram could set her free.

She was a silent stranger...to the grounds of
Lanka's palace,
Trapped in a cage wearing Lord Ram's ring,
And bearing with Ravan's malice.
The way she lived with simplicity,
defined the term grace,

She lived a life for her love,
truth was what she did embrace.
She lived without Lord Ram for so many days,
Without him she lived so long,
She knew in her heart she only loved him, though
others called her immoral and wrong.

She was a Goddess to the earth,
She made the soil pure by becoming its part,
She was a princess for her name...
but a Goddess for her heart.
Yet she never left her love for her Lord,
her sacrifices remain a witness,
The courage hidden in her charming nature...
made her a true Goddess.
She fought a silent war with love, with the strength
of her mind and skill,
She never let any other hamper her, change her
decision or will.
Folding hands with respect to her, bowing down to
her grace only,
How she lived a life with faith and loyalty,
embraced the truth gracefully.
And that is why Goddess Sita, Goddess Sita I stan,
For she was a woman with the will power of a man.

6.

No Belief Held in Endings

Each day brings a new morning,
and each day a new beginning,
Each day we start with something
with a hope to excel in.
A fire never burns into ending,
it only tires and comes to rest,
The simple way to start off each day
like the heart beats in our chest.
A butterfly never ends; it only sleeps until
it gives birth to new wings,
And then it gets back to flying again,
for no belief held in endings.

A span of life never ends, only souls
and bodies change,
We keep living on everyday; it's nothing
odd or strange.
A story too never ends; the ending of
it is what we decide.
Like the world is never ending, it maybe round
but it is wide,
There is no end to one's love,
for why lovers wear rings.
It is only the change of their hearts and minds,
for no belief held in endings.

We only have something to begin with;
even what we call an end is a start,
Like it starts afresh each day—
the blood pumping in our heart.

It is only the phrases that we use or the way
we term these things,
But for a hopeful one like me, there is
no belief held in endings.
Time as we know is eternity, you can't buy it from a shop,
Or a journey too never ends until
we decide to make it stop.
We begin each day with a fresh essence,
New born passion and zeal a beginning brings,
We only start or come to rest,
for no belief held in endings.

MARILYN
MONROE
ROLLING STONES
sucking in the seventies

7.

The Attic of Memories

As I found myself going through,
going through the old attic,
I went up slowly with a little fear, removing
the cobwebs with a stick,
Rather I whistled my way in, so that
I wouldn't feel scared,
But to see dolls with twitching eyes,
I wasn't really prepared.

There were dolls with shattered teeth,
And a broken smile which made them
rather sad; I felt petrified
Knowing these were the kind of dolls,
kids from those days had.
I see a book with pages glued by rust,
with a difficult to pronounce word,
A walkman from the 1980s with songs
from a band I've never heard,
An empty wine bottle with a fishy odour
and a fancy label,
A black and white television with lost buttons
and a broken cable.
The harness of a young child, a lace draped corset,
A broken glass cover on a
Rolling stones cassette.

Posters of Marilyn Monroe and a picture
signed by Audrey Hepburn,
And many couplets by speare, that were beauty
yet hard to learn.
A mirror covered with spiders but studded
with an emerald stone,
Does it realise since how many ages
it has been left alone?
Newspapers from the slavery times,
kept on a table with a lining of black gold,
A thick book of bedtime tales,
grandmother never told.
Pictures from the hidden routes,
articles on the silk trade,
A wooden clock and a rusty radio,
not used for over a decade,
A vintage radio that doesn't work and a pretty clock
that doesn't tick,
As I found myself going through,
going through the old attic.

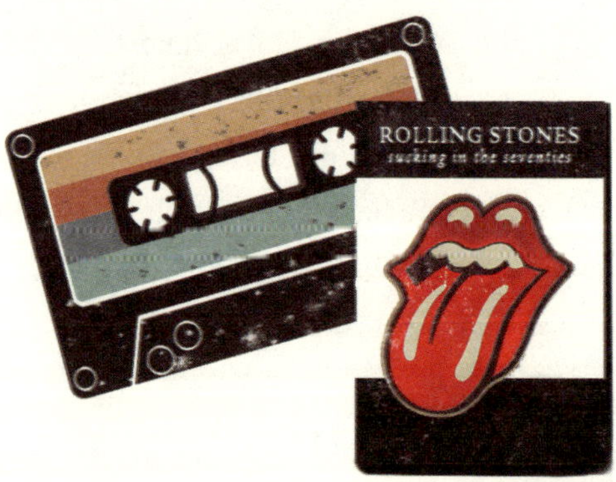

8.

Those Filmy Dreams Of Mine

Those filmy dreams of mine,
Make me want to catch a moving train,
They make me want to roll in the grass,
And don't care about being wet in the rain!
They make me want to let my hair loose,
To let a gun recoil;
They make me want to be left alone,
Alone with the winter soil;
They make me want to meet someone special
On the top of the Empire State;
They make me ponder on a meeting—
Was it a coincidence or fate?

They make me want to call from a phone booth
On a rainy afternoon;
They make me want to chase the sun and
Fall in love with the moon.
They make me want to have some stories to tell,
For when I grow old and fine,
Some are crazy, some are silly...
Those filmy dreams of mine!

9.

Honey, Promises Are Meant For Breaking

The silence of a fragmented heart is way
Louder than a yell.
For to say something the tongue may refuse, but the
Silence of the fragments can easily tell.
The heart divides itself into fragments,
For it is tired as a whole by aching.
But how many times shall it remind itself, honey,
Promises are meant for breaking.
The sorrow of a broken promise,
Each fragment does claim,
Though the pain felt in each fragment,
Is more or less the same.
To break a heart into fragments, to leave a heart broken
It is for what promises are meant
To leave an imprint on the heart...young and innocent.

The heart divides itself into fragments...for how long
Can it hold itself together aching?
And how many times shall it remind itself?
Honey...promises are meant for breaking.

10.

Bitten by the Rose

What a poet truly falls for, to the eye
A charming sight,
Yet only pretty to look at, if you touch,
It will bite.
It declares the taste of romance,
It is what the lover adorns,
Yet it may seem sly, for even the
Rose has thorns.

The poet who wants to fall in love,
But with an unfinished prose,
For a poet who is lovestruck,
Must be bitten by the rose.

11.

Princess of the Forest

Green emeralds which were rather eyes,
That shone like the northern lights;
A face as bright and symmetrical,
As the full moon in the darkest nights;
Cheeks that had a cherry flush,
A charming little nose with a diamond pin;
A bun with curly strands falling out,
And a charming brown mole down her chin.

She was a princess from a castle,
The princess that ran away;
For away into simplicity, deep into the forest
She wanted to stay.
She doesn't feel the need to come back,
For she lives in the home of a tree,
The branches provide her home,
The birds sing to her sweetly.

Now there in the forest, she doesn't feel alone,
For the waterfall becomes her royal bath,
The flowers provide her cologne.
The birds, the branches, the trees are her friends,
They protect her from danger,
But in the forest, she doesn't have any,
For none there is a stranger.

In nature's laps, in nature's arms,
A new world she does witness,
She is looked after by the forest,
By the forest Goddess.
Often when she sits in the tree trunk,
She looks like a bird in her nest,
The tree turning into a palace for the,
The princess of the forest.

12.

That of the Masquerade

Many a delightful faces, their beguiling dresses
And accents strike,
Dancing together like they are lovers,
Yet they don't know what the other looks like.
Faces remain a mystery, they don't
Let the suspense fade,
In a ball where mystery is cherished,
That of the masquerade!
They can't see the look one holds
In their face hence can't see the look of their heart.
They keep dancing either the waltz or
To an eminent Mozart,
Only there is to listen and dance, none to really stair
Only one night you can love under,
Under the glass chandelier.
A romance only embracing one's grace
Rather a game well played.
In a ball where mystery is cherished,
That of the masquerade.

13.

Books Kept in the Shelves

Whenever I wanted to visit, visit the land of elves,
I picked one of the mystical books kept in the shelves.
Exceptional it is how easily we could transport ourselves
To the land of elves,
Just by flipping those mystical pages by ourselves.

But in the times of computer screens...books in the shelves who reads?
When every book is on the computer,
A paper book who needs?
But this is the way it is, today's kids won't know
The magic of those books kept in the shelves.
The ones that we used to use to visit the land of elves.

14.

Blaue Augen

Blue eyes that struck purple lightning in my heart,
they were magical, reflective, and blue.
They were breathtakingly beautiful and the one who had them too.
To describe them, I can't use a flower; blue flowers are rare.
But what is enough to depict, I could see the Rhine falls in there.
Blue eyes that could bring out sweet emotions,
remind you of unspoken desires,
That carry the depth of mysterious seas and the
beauty of unheated sapphires.
Blue eyes that struck purple lightning in my heart,
they were magical, reflective, and blue.
They were breathtakingly beautiful and the one who had them too.

15.

Ocean Blue

There's a teardrop in the middle of the ocean;
No, it didn't fall from the sky,
Rather it fell from this ocean blue eye.
An ocean of tears rests in this eye,
And that is why it is so blue,
Lost a family she belonged to, lost her love that was true.
Blue eyes are blue for the sorrow they hold,
With every tear pouring, a dark secret unfolds.

Soaked, wet eyelashes, teardrops racing down the chin,
With every tear that fell down, the colour became thin.
The blue in her eyes which was once at its peak
Was now thin, thin white and weak.

Her sorrow had been swallowed by the ocean,
Perhaps by each teardrop that she poured,
The ocean gained its colour blue, hence sorrow was adored.

That is what gave the ocean its colour so blue
The story I tell you, majestic and true.

16.

Eyes

Several thousand faces
Are reflected in these eyes each day,
But only a few with a pursuit to stay.
Several thousand emotions these eyes may pertain,
Some are short lived, some forever remain.
The doorway to the world of emotional ability,
Life may thrive as long as these eyes are open to see,

Eyes can make you feel without contact of touch,
For they are gems in pursuit, I like to call them such.
They come in beautiful colors brown, green and blue,
They give you a chance to feel the world too.

17.

The Mystery in Her Eyes

Her eyes so clear, so beautiful; they captured
The haze and the mystery of the December fog.
Yet they were so clear, I could see my reflection in them.

The endless mystery dissolved;
In those eyes had somewhat a dark impression.
Yet to uncover and read those eyes, my utter desperation.

The more I tried to look through them, only the lesser I could see,
For in those mysterious eyes,
I could only perceive a reflection of me.

18.

God

All the galaxies in his palms, none that doesn't know him,
From the grace of life to the face of death,
the journey we all owe him.
The creator of the world we live in, the creator of the universe;
With his respect, with his love, we chant every verse.
His grace, his hand upon us is always everywhere.
We may not be able to see him, but he is always there.

As he grants life to a little child, he grants life to the bud on a tree
As he granted a life to you, he too granted a life to me.
As he created the colourful world with red, pink and blue
He coloured every little being; yes, that's true.
For our good deeds, he gives us presents through the people we know.
He puts us through situations that help us evolve and grow.
He has something for each he has created, for he brings joy to all;
Granting gifts to the ones succeeding,
Granting guidance to the ones that fall.
The birds of music, the birds of prey, the galaxies,
The planets he did create,
Words can't describe his magic, the almighty is great.

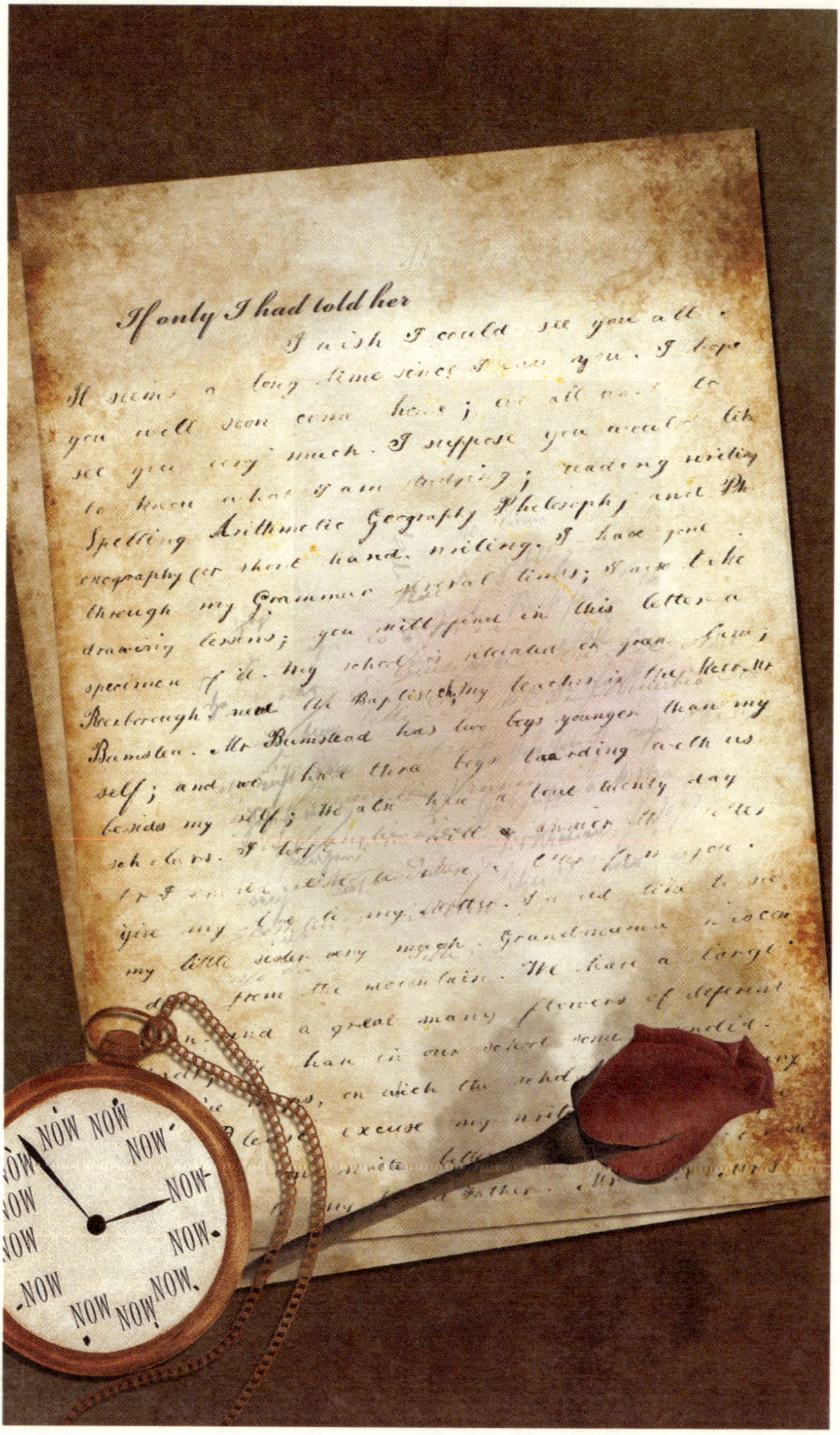
If only I had told her
NOW NOW NOW NOW NOW NOW NOW NOW NOW NOW NOW NOW

19.

Once Told, Forever Untold

Once told, forever untold...
Feelings that are a burden of suppression
Once told, forever untold,
So make it while you can: the confession.
Happiness, joy, peace, relief, seldom you will find,
Not for having confessed, what concerns your mind.
For if you confess while you have time,
You will receive a relieved impression,
Once told, forever untold,
So make it while you can... the confession.

20.

Entity in the Woods

Sometimes when I wander into the black woods,
I meet a mystical entity.
Something about her tells me so, she doesn't belong
To the same world as me.
Upon her when falls my gaze, it doesn't seem to stand,
I hold a precious piece in her that no one can understand.
Ah! The moon formed her face and the stars formed her wings,
For her feet leave behind stardust and her hair are spun
Of golden strings.
However, she may never leave the woods,
And would meet me in the woods only.
I wonder from which galaxy she comes, that mystical entity.

02
CHAPTER
Storytelling

21.

Nocturnal Badminton

The sky, layered by the blanket of the stars and the moon,
The doors locked, eyes closed swiftly, not to be opened soon,
Yet in the deep of the night, an estranged desire arose,
For I couldn't wait for the day,
My racket, lonely in the room, tempted me more to play.

I fastened my shoe-laces, held my racket & shuttle,
Heading to the park,
The night, still so silent, still pretty dark.
To my loneliness I thought, for none was there in my sight,
Just a fence and a racket; I had not a torch nor light.

To my racket, the shuttle for self I served across the fence so free,
A shadow as if someone served...for another serve I could see.
So excited I was for a companion that my astonishment I ignored,
Just playing with my racket, for playing was what I adored.

After countless serves, finally, curiosity bothered me.
Across the fence,
Who must be this fellow companion, playing badminton
at a night intense?
As I walked up across the fence, no shadow, no companion
I could see,
The one that stood there on the silent night were
Only my racket and me.

22.

At a Dark Station

At a dark station on a stormy night,
I stood waiting for the rain to settle.
Just then the station master headed towards me,
With an old lantern and a kettle.
He said in a slow voice: Sire, the train
would arrive much later for it still has to pass that narrow ark,
The driver must have had a little trouble
in the narrow turn for it was pretty rainy and dark.

He asked me to come some other day,
For I won't reach on time to my destination,
I knew that the weather would delay the journey,
Then why was I waiting at the station?
I didn't pay him heed, for I believed the weather would be better,
However, as I stood there and waited...
It got even darker and wetter.

Thirst bothered me as I saw, saw the handpump being
pulled by a wrench,
As I listened in on the gossip of two porters,
Seated on a bench.
I got bored as I waited but I saw something
Which wasn't there a while ago,
A man in a black ensemble, selling boiled sweet potato.

I had no one to talk to there so
I went forward to make some mates,
The potato seller served me with a sweet smile,
Wooden toothpicks and paper plates.

As I sat and ate, we talked about the rain delaying
the train from another hill,
Though he didn't complain for due to the pitter-patter,
We could avoid the crows shrill.

He asked where I was off to so late, for the train
passed through hills so steep,
I told him to visit my aunt in the hills and
That through the journey I would simply sleep.

A young girl then broke our converse,
to sell flowers which she had fetched.

I told her I'd like one for my aunt as
my black leather wallet stretched
I gave her a few extra coins to fill her little piggy bank,
And told her to play with paper boats,
play with them until they sank.
As the three of us sat and shared ideas,
Time passed by pretty fast,
And then I heard the crushing of the stones and pebbles,
Oh, it had come at last.
The station master gave me a call,
as I ran to my coach's opening door,

I sat on the seat marked in my ticket,
Waving goodbye to the mates on the station floor.
I waved to the potato seller, I waved to the flower girl.
I waved to the pitter-patter I heard from the sky,
As the engine set off once again into the hills.
The train waved goodbye.

23.

Take Me Someplace

Take me someplace in the morning bloom,
From where we return before dusk of the day.
Take me someplace you'd want to go,
Take me someplace far away.
Take me someplace where peace knocks,
A place that you would like to see,
Just take me someplace which you would desire,
Our destination doesn't matter to me.

Take me someplace humid and still,
Where a stream does flow.
Take me someplace far away, where you'd like to go.
Take me someplace far away...so far away,
That we must drive across meadows.
Take me someplace where in the day, the shiny moon glows.

But if you want to keep driving...
Keep driving through the highway.
But take me someplace you'd want to go,
Take me someplace far away.

24.

The Swings

As the gushing wind pushes my body,
To push myself as fast I try;
To push my feet forward so that like a bird I can fly.
As the wind rushes through the gaps within the steel strings,
I can feel my body floating,
As I yield to my invisible wings.

I feel the inner bird in me that eagerly waits to depart,
From the nest to the outer world,
It yearns to fly out her heart.
My invisible wings, my inner bird, my passion to fly it brings,
For when I want to feel the bird, I sit and ride the swings.

25.

The Lone Pianist

The pianist lone at night, practising in a dark hall,
For he has to prepare well to present a performance at the ball.
But not to any other shadow,
Only to the piano he does belong,
For he keeps playing it again and again,
The keys to his favourite song.
The only way to find him is if you carefully stare,
But you wouldn't even realise, not even his shadow is there.

The only way to feel his presence,
Is to listen to what he plays,
Even if it keeps playing the same song for days.
You can't see him in the darkness,
But only hear piano playing in the moonlight shawl.
The pianist lone at night, practising in a dark hall.

26.

Into My Kitchen

The odour of the roasted garlic,
Ripping apart the stitched onion peel,
As I cook up another story in my warm pot of steel.
I roast the peanuts warm, with little jaggery and dates,
As they toast...I clean them white, the silver forks and plates.
Shavings of parmesan and blocks of English cheddar,
Which one shall I sprinkle on my salad today?
I may look for some guidance,
Listen to what the recipe book has to say.
Then I clean the meat, I wash it...to then marinate,
To make a pot meal, a mouth-watering plate.
I save now the warm nuts for my cold dessert,
And take a look at what has been cooking up in the hearth,
For now, my curry is done, I inhale the feel,
The story cooked in my warm pot of steel.

27.

Braided My Hair

The one who braided my hair,
Ran her fingers through them like silk strands,
The scent of mustard oil,
The grease from churned butter in her hands.
Her fingers slipped through my hair,
As she combed leisurely with a wooden brush,
The comb moved so slow yet her chatter continued...
For we were never in a rush.

On her way back from the temple...she would
pick the fallen Mogra,
Placing them in warm water, from which she'd
scent my strands.
She would press my forehead,
And strengthen my hair with the firmness of her hands.

My hair like silk yet fluffy as cotton,
Never I learned how to braid,
For, from my childhood to my youth,
She was the one who had them made.
She went slow...so she could complete
a tale of faraway fantasy,
The one that left her scent, in my braided hair for me.

28.

The Cuckoo in Our Neighbourhood

Breathing into the soul of aurora,
Pumping life into it all,
Resonates with the silence of the breeze,
That ringing sweet call.
As the first ray of the sun pierces the clouds,
She pierces the silence as she should,
Sounding as sweet as the laughter, that of a new born baby would.

She has a tiny framework, with eyes popping out like gloss,
She wakes me up in the break of the day,
With her sweet little chaos.
She sings with grace free of lyrics but with her own melody,
Yet the glory of her tone suggests,
She understands rhythm better than me.

She calls out to children, to wake up for school,
And sings to their father's snore,
In such a beautiful voice that we so yearn for more.
She gives us a taste of her melody, like a renowned artist would,
But oh! Did I forget to mention?
She is the artist of our neighbourhood.
She wakes up earlier than most of us, so we are early awake,
For being our littler saviour, credit she doesn't take.
To set her as my telephone tone, oh I really wish I could,
The one gifted truly with a voice,
The cuckoo in our neighbourhood.

29.

Waiting for the Postman

When my chores are over, I sit by alone
Under the creaking fan,
Waiting eagerly for him to come, waiting for the postman.
In the youth of the morning tranquillity,
I sit in the garden humming,
Waiting for this day since a while, for the postman is coming.
Who must have remembered me now?
Who must write this letter to me?
My heart surrenders to patience, waiting for him eagerly.

May it be my family or the one my dreams await,
May it be a letter of love, charming me into a date.
I wonder who they may be, for I expected a letter from some,
That is why I was waiting in with fervour, for the postman to come.

I don't want to keep waiting long, my patience doesn't grant allowance.
For to read my letter, I adore the verve of a child's innocence.
To not await the postman, my spirit couldn't or can
Waiting eagerly for him to come...waiting for the postman.

30.

Arrow in the Eye

An arrow in the eye, aced with great dedication,
The way he carved his goal, gives us great motivation.
When others were the ones to observe the trees,
To observe the sun, to observe the sky,
He became the only one...the only one who observed the eye.
As he pulled off the string, the arrow and the eye met,
It shows us what he truly observed was none but his target.
He was the archer of the night...blinded by his goal,
Who left the bird blind by carving the eye whole.

To pave a way for his goal, so no distraction could swirl him away,
Only into the eye of the bird, that is where his eye did lay.
For we should look only into our goals...
not into the distractions, why?
Then I will always tell you, prince Arjun's arrow in the eye.

31.

If a Thought Can Change Your Life

If a thought can change your life, you shall think good,
If you believe kindness is a charm, use it as you should.
Treat others well, the same way they would treat you,
Never scorn one's struggle,
Who knows what they are going through?

Like the moon you shall keep calm,
Like the sun keep warm and bright,
You can control your own temper...before it controls you, right?
The ones in our remembrance, only their goodness has stood,
If a thought can change your life, you shall think good.

32.

Fly O Little Bird

The little bird in her mother's nest, peeking at the sky,
But if she always remains afraid, how would she learn to fly?
Race with the wind, race with the kites,
Make new friends and reach new heights.

If only in a little nest with her mother she would be,
How beautiful how enchanting the world is,
she wouldn't ever see.

To fly and go far away, she could only yearn,
For if she never tries, how would she ever learn?
Only if she seeks her mother's nest to peek at the sky,
Mother should tell her that to learn, the only way is to try,
For if she ever wants to explore the world, she only can by flying,
But could she ever do so, if she is afraid of trying?

33.

A Train With No Destination

Mesmerising, the scenery from a train,
Passing through the coasts of Italy, the coasts of Spain.
Passing through the Swiss Alps, passing through
The streets of Greece.
Passing through Venice in Italy; in France, Nice.

The light at the end of each dark tunnel unveils a new destination,
Neither a stop nor a station.
Unlike the speedy Eurostar, this train is slow to go,
For it has plenty of cities, plenty of countries to show.

Be it the scorching pyramids of Giza,
Or Toronto where it likes to snow.
The journey itself igniting temptation,
The mesmerising train with no destination.

34.

Dil Se (from the heart)

Embracing a black overspread sitting quietly,
Not a sound to be heard in miles...Haflong station.
Got a matchstick? I cried from a distance,
To light my cigar in temptation.
Not an acknowledgement, I did receive,
For I thought he was a man, he must have one I believed.
The moon shone so bright, yet so dark, yet so deserted,
I kept asking for the matchstick yet no one reverted.
But the wind was restless, restless and curious to show me,
To show who was sharing the station with me that night,
For it lifted that overspread, rather that veil,

Only to reveal a woman in sight.
A woman I gasped, my asking for a
matchstick now wouldn't seem so right.
As soon as I flashed my gaze upon her...to catch a glimpse of her face,
She hurried and covered herself again, with much beauty and grace.
Excuse me! Would you have a matchstick? I muttered.
But she wasn't one for acknowledgement,
Yet my desire to speak to her got more restless, rather vehement.
I'll tell you my name, no need to tell me yours...I said.
I talked to that mysterious beauty with a veil over her head,
I blathered, I pleaded...
She was quiet, not heeded.
After a while of listening to myself converse...
I heard another voice...one cup of warm tea it murmured,
My mind & my heart obeyed this voice,
Finally, she said something by her choice.
I told her, please don't move, please don't go,
I'll have myself back in a minute to show.
I hustled in the rain to the tea stall close by.

My red jacket was my umbrella,
Two cups of hot tea, I said to the fella,
Be quick, I cried, and helped him pour the tea,
Obeying the only words, the mysterious beauty had said to me.
As the tea was being prepared, a familiar sound I heard,
The train was departing, this fact to me occurred,
I was handed over the cups of tea and again I raced through the rain,
But this time only to find the beauty in the veil,
Heading elsewhere in the train.

35.

Village Storyteller

The village storyteller he is, listen to the stories he tells.
Not just heaps of fun but wisdom and knowledge he sells.
He wanders from village to village and sits under a tree,
To share the wonderful stories he captured in his journey.
He writes about the people he meets,
Or about how a fool met intelligence;
But each story that he tells captures pure innocence.

A charmer amongst the children of the villages, he is said.
For his stories amuse and inspire, telling them to move ahead.
The men of the village hence call him a man with a fine mind,
For each story he tells is truly a golden find.
Not rings of gold or silver but a whole treasure he sells,
The village storyteller he is, listen to the stories he tells.

36.

Dancing in an Empty Palace

Dancing in an empty palace, dancing on my toes,
Dancing to my knees,
Dancing if I am the only one, myself I have to please.
Dancing like a carefree bird in the sky,
Like I am the only one around;
In a palace so empty, I can feel my every breath,
I can feel my every sound.

Dancing to my own muse, dancing to my own song,
None to judge me, none to call me wrong.
Professing to the gentleman of my dreams, who I want to romance,
Could I feel my heart beat tempting to pursue him to a dance?
I could feel my heart racing, I could feel my heart panting,
I could feel the intoxication in the air...Ooh, it was enchanting.
The calm, the empty: my wonderland and I the dancing Alice,
For if I were to find a place to dance, it would be an empty palace.

37.

Simplicity of Life

Happiness adorned in the simplicity of life,
It's in the simplest moments of all that we find joy,
Spending time with loved ones or the innocence of playing with a toy,
Going out to a movie, a play or relishing a favourite meal,
Meditating to the silence of time, listening to music that would heal.

Owning a much-desired ornament or a much-desired attire,
Peeking inside the heart, a beloved face to admire.
Humming with the nightingale, sitting under a tree
The biggest joy, the biggest happiness,
Is often found in life's simplicity.

03
CHAPTER

Nature

38.

Silent Calls from Woodland

The subliminal silence of the woodland,
As if to me it calls
The silence of the woodland,
Can be heard through the concrete walls
The calls of the woodland are silent such,
Calling me as if so, inviting me much,
The silence so silent is drawing me thus.

For behind it rests a world that doesn't belong to us.
Yet its silence somewhere leads to exaltation,
To uncover that world, a strong urge, a temptation.
The silence is silent, yet I have eagerness to see,
For the silence of the woodland calls to me.

39.

A Dewy Evening

I sit still in an offbeat cafe, sipping on malt cold brew.
As the glass beside my seat starts to sip on the dew.
I look at the time on my watch as I look at the pouring drop,
It's been an hour or so, but the pouring wouldn't stop.

As I feel my hope sinking away with the rain,
The hope to see the clouds drive away.
As the day set into an evening bloom,
I wonder how long the weather will make me wait today.

I even forgot to bring my umbrella,
But not my wallet with a change of tens,
I tossed and caught them before sketching a scenery,
With my mini sharpie pens.

Drawing a little scenery from what I see through
The dewy glass on a paper tissue,
Of the rain which is beautiful, though a trouble,
Though an issue.

As the sun is slowly going down,
I sit still but with an empty glass of brew,
Yet the glass beside my seat is still sipping on the dew.

40.

The Rain Is Coming

The clouds bestow upon the skies, young hearts are humming,
The peacocks flutter their plumes, for the rain is coming.
As young batsmen distress so,
To gather the clothes outside their mothers are running,
The crops are set to meet a heavy treat, for the rain is coming.

Two hearts sharing an umbrella wearing galoshes so stunning,
The child is ready to jump in puddles, for the rain is coming.
The grass tempts so eagerly as much as the bare river running,
The taste yearning for warm fritters and tea, for the rain is coming.

Fragrant the soil, fragrant the woods, fragrant the earth is becoming,
Hearts beheld, eagerness is adorned, for the rain is coming.

41.

When It Rains in the Forest

The frogs race in the slippery soil,
As the birds head for a shelter in their nest.
The snakes coil up in the tree trunks, when it rains in the forest.
Somewhere under the wet ground, rabbits find shelter to hide,
As the wet tracks outside either float away,
Or get blocked with the landslide.
A dance performed by the mythically enchanting plumage,
That of the shiny blue breast,
For it only welcomes with gratification when it rains in the forest.

The deer stops in the woods, it is raining it knows,
The river which was rather dry, now like an ocean it flows.
The soil turns into mud, and the holes in the trunks the water fills;
Though it doesn't seem to bother the ones in the ant hills.
The snails come out for a stroll, in the mud their shell floats,
But predators choose to remain indoors, like the foxes and the coyotes.
As the bear heads to a den, the vultures come in for getting rinsed,
The adobe filled with water, yet the rain isn't convinced.
The leaves absorb the scent, the scent of the raindrops
But the bats badly want it to, want the rain to stop.

The trees and their leaves feel enlightened,
For the rain makes them feel the freshest.
Though the tulip flowers close their cheeks when it rains in the forest,
Just the pouring of the scotch mist
Is enough to unlock the conduct of nature's quest,
For the nature has its own roles when it rains in the forest.

42.

Beaches

Coconut milk poured in a bright pineapple slice,
Flesh of the rosy lychees poured in citrus ice,
Cinnamon dusted over schnapps of fresh Californian peaches,
With juicy melting lobster rolls, buttery crab cakes served at beaches.

The stronger the sun, the cooler the breeze,
Coconuts hanging brown on the tall palm trees.
The only muse, the fierce waves, bring in a sense of calm,
As the shade of the trees offer the perfect summery balm.
The slippery withering sand dissolving with the waves,
The strange, amusing way, the nature behaves.
My gaze through the hat stops at the waves,
Yet stops to wave at each,
The waves, the sun, the trees, the visions of the beach.

43.

Of the Trees

Tall, bushy, branchy and wide, their leaves blowing with the breeze,
Providing us with various benefits, the beautiful tall trees.
Their beauty worth admiring, beautiful yet useful too,
Proving more beneficial with their growth, their service loving and true.

They give us oxygen, give us paper, and give us good medication,
They give us wood to build our homes and for furniture creation.
They provide fruits and flowers and are home to nests,
They make home for the wilderness; they help form the forests.
To us they give so much, floating with the moving breeze,
Providing us with various benefits, the beautiful tall trees.

44.

Majestic Mashobra

Violet flowers falling, falling from the tree branches onto my neck,
Exhausting yet breathtaking, the ethereal Mashobra trek.
Relishing a delightful shorba by the enchanting waterfall,
A cup of tea and spicy chickpea at a cute tea stall.

The solitude of the peaks, contrasting the packed campsites,
Tourists from Delhi and Mumbai in awe
of the constellation covered nights,
Orchards of apple in the Himalayan provinces we please,
Astounding views and the cool breeze,
The bustling markets, a shopping spree,
At the majestic Mashobra there is a lot more to see.

45.

Nature's Sweet Romance

The flute of the snake charmer which the snake can't resist,
It dances with grace, matching each note with a twist.

When they hear the sound of the honey dew raindrops,
They stop by to dance, the gorgeous peacocks.

And when the nearby cuckoo sings, we look outside and glance,
Transforming into a tale of nature's sweet romance.

46.

Swinging Waves

The ocean waves swing into the sky,
dissolving with the clouds, beyond they slip,
Like waves of water, slashing through a marshmallow dip.
The wonders that the ocean can do, leaving science confused,
Leaving the painters, the artists all of them amused.
Isn't it how we describe, magic in the songs that we sing?
But never did we know how far the ocean waves can swing.

The ocean it holds pearls and power, yet holds much calm in its fist,
For when the clouds feel the ocean, they soften into pleasures of mist.
The clouds become cotton balls, the waves, a sullen tide,
The cotton slowly drowns in the water,
the clouds melt as they collide.

It melts and dissolves into the clouds
as it first fills them with its watery grip,
And when the clouds start drowning like cotton,
they turn into mist and slip.
The waves swing to the clouds far away, to make them into mist of the day,
But as the cotton always falls for, the clouds too always fall and trip,
The ocean waves that touch the sky, dissolving with the clouds,
And beyond they slip.

47.

Something about Wildlife

There is something about wildlife, we all must understand,
They may seem to live on the same, but belong to foreign land.

We are strangers to the forest, we must leave it alone,
The animals don't need us, they like to be on their own.
We mustn't intrude their privacy as we don't like ours to be intruded.
The forest is their home, where we are strangers not included
We only like to chase them with our flashing cameras and jeeps,
We bother them for our own fun, act as intruders and creeps.

We are never ashamed of our actions...
their skin, their fur we are wearing,
And then we act surprised and wonder,
wonder why they are disappearing.
We keep cutting down the woods,
build more homes and buildings near,
But don't we realise, somebody already lives here.

We ruthlessly exploit the benefits we get,
animals can never be our friends,
Because the lust in the soul of a human,
the greed of a human never ends

Deep in the forest to promote hunting,
we built a pathway and a road,
We know them well but don't want to follow

the rules of nature's abode
We only want to satisfy our desires...
give into the greed in our hand,
Not everything made by God belongs to us we must understand.

Even if it requires torturing them, it is something we would still do,
Because we don't care about them and it is what we want to.
We don't bother to leave them alone
even when they are held in captivation,
We forget that we are animals too, we don't own god's every creation.

We make truck drivers go through forest routes
in nights of their brandy tass,
They drive recklessly, without caution, care for the animals that pass.

Through the habitat of an animal's child, we carve a train track,
We take from even if little they have, in an animal child's sack.
We take their pictures, we take their lives, and we take their skin,
There is no category or task, we may spare them in.

From the clutches of our cruelty, they have never been freed,
In the world where humans are more, hence endless is the greed.
They are only innocent beings which we humans punish,
Because we want each to serve us and live according to our wish.

We must treat them like we treat a human for they are not any different,
To make the world colourful and aesthetic,
these creatures from god were sent.
We must leave them to who they are, leave them to the foreign land,
There is something about wildlife, we all must understand.

48.

Hills in My Heart

A brown hill wearing a wedding gown of tall and tall conical trees,
A place which welcomes tourists just like it
welcomes fountains of breeze.
As you go up the shying hill, the white snow is her silk tulle veil,
And the waterfalls are tears of her anticipation,
which steer reflections just as fresh steel.
Spicy and woody is the scent of the trees that
look like upside down ice cream cones,
As they circle around the waterfall as its white
water ripples along silver greyish stones.
Pretty roads are knotted around the hill like
flowers on her wedding gown,
And for that boy on the bicycle,
who lives somewhere near the quiet town,
There's a cute way to cycle beside the peaceful lake,
a warm slice of pizza to eat,
And for those who enjoy shopping a bit more,
there's an elite luxury street.
The ribbons on her gown of gingerbread like
homes make the view a sight to please,
A brown hill wearing a wedding gown of tall and tall conical trees ...

49.

Saturn

With a gorgeous ring it rests, golden brown inclining
Far away from us, yet we can see it shining.
Comets, asteroids, chunks of broken ice invented,
The rings from the moons that shine though fragmented.
An iridescent round ball with a ring as a pattern,
Mystical, magnificent, the beautiful Saturn.

50.

Somewhere Along the Fjords

Somewhere along the fjords, tremendous diffusion of hail.
Somewhere along the fjords, where imposing ships set sail.

Inside a warm bistro, grilled salmon so juicy, silken & tender,
Grilled then glazed, with honey and lavender.

Outside would be a tremendous diffusion of snowflakes,
Fleets of ice surrounding the fjords, glaciers gracing the lakes.
Fjords surrounded by icebergs, patched by the frosted rolls,
Often irresistibly drawn I am towards the mysterious trolls.
This country seemingly from a movie, from a classic folk tale,
A beautiful sherbet of ice, tremendous diffusion of hail.

As I ride upon the slippery wet roads on my blue tricycle,
Falling from the blue branches of trees are crystal blue icicles,
Once more to see a tremendous diffusion of snowflakes,
Platters of cheese, sausages, wine and steaks.

This country, this place, a crystal blue ray,
Frozen yet resplendent, majestic Norway.

51.

Fireflies

Born as if from the sun, shining bright like its ray,
Bringing light to the nights, resting in the peace of the day.
Like flying stars, circling us around,
In the darkest of corners, their radiance is found.
Oh, I so do wish I could capture them in silver jars,
Dominate them like the sun, these radiant flying stars.

Oh, I so do wish I could capture them in my palms,
But never to release in the skies,
These radiant like sun, yet cool like stars,
These burning fireflies.

52.

Eye of the Tiger

The beings belonging to the woodland vast;
To charm us yet create a terror they are able
For emerging they are from the wilderness, calm and formidable.
For utmost passion, fierce anger relies in their glimmering jaws,
The temptation resting in the blood
From the eyes follows to the restless paws.

The rulers they are of the woodland, yet only ruling at night,
For in the night hunting a prey, in the day not a sight.
Yet not a mystery they are, for all over the land their trace,
The pug marks left in the lustrous ooze, effortlessly with grace.

Their saffron fur, velvet essence coming to light, gracing the dark,
Ruling around the luscious woodlands of the famous national park.
Rest wherever, they leave essence to the orbit,
Feeling their sense, feeling their essence, feeling the tigers of Corbett.

53.

Oh! A World Like That

Oh, would a world like that, ever be able to manifest?
When the birds are free to swim in the sky, the ocean is pure at its best.
When the humans would let free the wild,
Never to perform a circus stunt.
The humans would leave big cats to poach,
Burn the desire to kill and hunt.
When the times would be changed so we wouldn't need a forest ranger,
The wilderness would rule freely without being in danger.

Why are humans cruel so? Why can't we just let them be?
Why to torture? Why to capture?
When we can leave them wild and free.
When the nature is blooming happily,
When the wilderness is free at rest,
Oh! Would a world like that ever be able to manifest?

54.

Moon River

The moon drowned into the river,
So soulfully, with elegance and grace,
When the river silently captured the charming moon's face,
The river fluttered with an unusual radiance,
As if highlighting the moon it held,
The night escalated into the darkest it had ever,
While only the shiny river bed dwelled.

An overpowering ambience the river had attained,
For now, not only a river it was but where the moon remained.
The river thought to self:
Now I will shine brighter than any ocean, any sea,
For now, the drowned shine of the universe,
The power of the night, resides in me.

55.

What Must He Think?

The birds I created for swiftly swimming across the skies,
Are being trapped in golden cages, leered at by curious eyes.
The plants and trees I created for breathing and giving shade,
Are being burnt down in fires, being cut down for trade.

The wilderness I created for living freely in containment,
Are trapped in cages, being used for entertainment.

The oceans, rivers I created for giving life to creatures, allowing them to feed,
Are being dirtied, polluted as if now not in need.
The humans I created to live in harmony,
nurture the land, nurture the sky
Are doing the obverse, I wonder why?

56.

All Along the Jungle Trail

The bumpy roads with muddy puddles, the land cruiser set sail,
Racing with little birds smoothly, all along the jungle trail.
The beauty of this place lies in its silence,
the rustling of the leaves a proof,
The fragrance of the gorgeous air seeping
through the unveiled sunroof.

Superior to any cologne, the forest fresh spoil,
Tilled, nurtured and born of the luscious fresh soil.
The music all of the journey, only calls of monkey and the nightingales,
Singing with them is me smoothly, all along the jungle trail.

04
CHAPTER
Memories

new york city
empire state building
BROADWAY
chrysler
upper east side
Brooklyn Bridge

57.

NYC

A city of business moving exceedingly fast,
One that stops for none, touching the clouds so vast.
A skyline taller than the sky,
Flanked by a stream of cars rushing by.
The central park, delightful and pretty,
Located in the heart, the centre of the city.

The Statue of Liberty, magnificent- the Statue of Liberty great,
The charmingly romantic Brooklyn Bridge,
The building of the Empire State.
The marvellous Manhattan; Times Square that doesn't sleep,
Lower east side Chinatown, wherein night doesn't creep.

Luxury homes, estates brought to light by the Long Island Sea,
Call it the Big Apple, the Goth Gotham or just the amazing NYC.

58.

Childhood Zeal

The cream floating on the surface, on the surface of the milky brew,
Now I wouldn't drink the tea, but that cream is what I'd like to chew.
When sushi would be ordered, I'd take the chopsticks for a craft,
I would stack them together with glue to make a wooden raft.

I'd crush the candy canes and put the powder in straw sets,
And then pretend to smoke strawberry, orange flavoured cigarettes.

I'd make a sterling sword from the lunch-box foil,
To fight the monsters under my bed,
And always do the opposite of what all my elder sister said.
I knew that it was time to return home,
When dogs under the street light began to bark,

Though the laughter and fun we had in the playgrounds,
Went on till the very dark.

I tied my cart to Timmy's cycle,
The cart which was an old shoe box with a rag.
I used to shout: "Faster Timmy," as the cart his cycle would drag.

I would become even more stubborn,
When my queries wouldn't get responded to,
For when I didn't get mother's attention,
Tantrums weren't something new.
When I remember all that fun now, nostalgia is what I feel,
Truly tempted by nostalgia, that of my childhood zeal.

59.

About Grandmother

Unending is its desire to feed, her passionately vigorous rolling pin,
To visit her house and not have lunch, for her is no less than a sin.
They always seem to never end;
the stories of her youth,
She tells you what they are all about,
but no one knows the truth.

In her house remain all your doodles and pictures of your childhood.
Her habit of reminding how mischievous you were,
spoiling you more than mother would.
Her house is filled with the smell of food and all things vintage;
As you ask her to show you pictures of when she was your age.
The most adorable she is, as well as the most fun,
Talking I am about grandmother hon!

60.

Mother Always Told Me

Mother always told me, told me to be good.
Told me to share love and kindness as much as I could.

Mother always told me when I would doubt in my head,
If I kept doubting myself, how would I move ahead.
Mother always told me, to my tests when I was scared,
She told me why would I need to be, for I am well prepared!

Mother always told me, told me when I wouldn't win,
Still wouldn't be no path or choice she wouldn't support me in.

Mother always told me, when I would succeed and slay,
I should keep going for hard work always does pay.
I would always remember, what my mother always told,
For the words she spoke weren't words but gold.

61.

Picnic

Danish strawberries dipped in molten chocolate,
Baked dough dipped in cheese fondue,
The finest of wine, the finest of olives, the warm pot of chicken stew.
Satin red raspberries along with the garlic buttered silky toasts,
Followed by the pastel blanket and women indulging in boasts.

Crawling over the lush green land, their little poodles doing tricks,
Yummy baskets, chatty women, cute poodles, and sweet picnics...

62.

Memories

How often they pass us by the memories, it is hard to keep track,
To give us joy or tears in our eyes, moments keep coming back.
Sometimes we laugh, sometimes we cry,
we owe it to the world we live in.
Sometimes we may not finish the race, sometimes we may win.
Memories keep us refreshed; yet take us back in time,
From now it is to when it was mine.

Though they make us cry, yet they make us smile,
That is why we hold them in our hearts, so intensely each while.
We may want to forget, yet would remain trapped in our treasury,
Could make us laugh, could make us cry, only a memory.

63.

An Idle Day

On a day when I sit calmly, to my tasks there is none so new,
I just wonder to myself, for there is nothing to do.
When I would just look at the waves as I sit back ashore,
Listening to the muse of the waves not feeling the need to bore.
When I would think about the adventures like a kid,
Realising a teen I am but many of them I haven't did.

How much energy the cheetah has? For so fast it does run,
More to wonder would be, how old must be the sun?
When I would just sit on the green grass and talk to the sky so blue,
On a day when I sit calmly, for there is nothing to do.

64.

Yet Feels Like Yesterday

When we would sit together and relish
snow cones in the scorching heat of May,
Wow, what a long time ago, yet feels like yesterday.
When the teacher would exclaim: 'Happy holidays,
Summer vacations begin from today!'
Wow what a long time ago, yet feels like yesterday.

When we would travel several hours on roads,
On the journey see cows chewing hay,
Wow, what a long time ago, yet feels like yesterday.
When we would visit cute markets to buy jewels of wooden and clay,
Wow, what a long time ago yet feels like yesterday.

When we circled around the banyan
tree to tell horror stories in the day,
Wow, what a long time ago, yet feels like yesterday.
When we said we would miss all this someday,
Now what we do, what we say
Wow, what a long time ago! Yet feels like yesterday.

65.

To Mother, With Love

There is no question I can ask her, that she doesn't know the answer to,
As if I have a mind of glass, she always seems to see through.
Even before I tell her, she knows the reason behind my smile.
She knows what brings the radiance in my eyes,
she reads my heart meanwhile.

Her love for me is an endless sea, that can never be measured,
Every little detail about her is something that is treasured.
She always keeps me inspired for she works from dawn to dark,
Being the perfect woman, being my hero, being my spark.

She works all day with no salary and says her salary is my smile,
Which keeps her motivated and makes it all worthwhile.

She teaches me some amazing things, some beautiful things in life,
To be a good mother to me; to be a good wife,
She is the fruit and I am the flower,
She has raised me to shine, to be a lover.

She puts me before any other; she loves me like no one can,
The love of a mother can't ever be compared even to the love of a man.

She'd always be honest with me, whether harsh or sweet,
She taught me to be independent, to stand up on my own two feet.
She becomes a cook, a teacher, a friend,
a counsellor and a lantern in the dark to me.

But to become and manage all these at once,
I sometimes wonder how can she?
She is the mother that I am lucky to have;
she is the mother that everyone needs,
My beautiful mother, my lovely mother,
for she does such magical deeds.

66.

Trojan Horse

Things aren't always what they seem.
That beautiful horse being great,
One that stood as a significance of cleverness
still blows me till date.

The war that was combated through ages
between the province of Greece and Troy,
Was celebrated when the Greeks surrendered
and the Trojans sought victory and joy.

When the Greeks seemingly surrendered,
left in the battlefield was only a wooden horse great,
The sheer beauty of the horse convinced the Trojans
to make it pass through their gate.
Soon at night the joyous Trojans fell into sweet sleep so fast,
Only for the mystery of the sleek wooden horse to be unravelled at last.

How beautiful that horse was, but looks can play deceit,
For the wooden horse released the Greeks led the Trojans' to defeat.
Things aren't always what they seem as the Trojans were to remorse,
For an army of Greeks were hiding all the while in that sleek wooden horse.

67.

Teacher

She is always the one to push us, to show us how far we can go,
The more she speaks, the more she tells,
the more we feel the lesser we know.
She shouldn't be celebrated for only a year but for many years to come,
For she may remain with you only for a while
but a lifetime will last her wisdom.

Though she has a passion to teach, she doesn't leave the passion of learning,
Some new discovery each day,
knowledge is for what her mind is yearning.
She is a book with pages that have only wisdom and knowledge to give,
For to teach is a gift, is a passion to live.

She is the one that becomes our mother,
becomes our mother at school,
She teaches us to be good, while keeping calm and cool.
But when we'd become mischievous and silly as we are,
Don't then we force her, force her to take away our star;?
She may scold us at times, but it is for our own good
She brings out in us the ability to learn more than anyone could.

Before becoming anything in life,
a good person is what she teaches us to be,
The potential we have hidden inside us, she helps to bring it out to see.
In the middle of a difficult sentence, when our voice breaks,
She helps us to move ahead and correct our mistakes.

She tells us to be a humble being in life, as we move up ahead.
One day when we'll need advice, we would remember what she said,
She may give us something a little tough but it is for us to learn.
But even sweetness is the hidden reason,
The hidden reason behind her being stern.

She says learning is a lifelong treat; earning knowledge does never stop,
For she wants to see all her students, all her students at the top.
Her love for us is strict it may seem, and so is the dedication in her,
The one that pushes us to be our best,
The golden soul of a teacher.

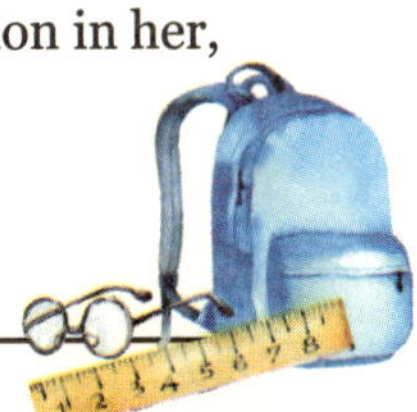

68.

A Friend of Mine from the Older Days

A friend not remembered in a while, a friend of mine from the older days,
Across the village of east town, a little far from the colony she stays.
Why I decided to remember her today, why not so...I did before?
For today I happened to find her pink handkerchief,
which she had once left at my door.

The friendships formed at school retire, retire after for different
journeys...friends depart,
Friends may not be together anymore, but
friendships are held in the heart.
Like my heart held her friendship, I'm sure she still holds mine,
I remember that she wanted to be an artist; I knew she wanted to shine.

I remember all that about her, by just seeing her little handkerchief,
A friend of mine with innocence in her eyes
but a heart filled with mischief.
I remember our little quarrels, weren't we like Tom and Jerry?
As I like to remember those memories, even our quarrels were merry.

I remember the game of snakes and ladders,
Why was it the one she'd always choose?
For it was that one golden game where only I had a chance to lose.
I remember how she put it under my desk, her old used bubble gum,
And she'd poke holes into my umbrella,
When she realised the rain would come.

Though her pranks bothered me, I was silent with what I did,
When in her backpack, a bunch of fake insects I hid!
I remember when we were in detention, we had fun even their,
We were careless, for even detention we wouldn't spare.

I remember the days clearly, to talk paper planes we sent,
With messages written in a code language,
Which only we knew what it meant,

I remember as too for it must have been some 20 years,
didn't I come to conclusion how
I wonder if she would have changed, what she must look like now
I look at her handkerchief as forgotten memories,
Forgotten memories from the older days.
A friend of mine not remembered in a while,
Across the east town she stays.

69.

Scotland

Strawberry shortcake and rolls compiled by yeast,
Empire biscuit, what an imposing yet classic feast.
A climate cool and wet, a climate gentle and calm,
The highlands of Scotland, of Scotland the farm!

The sight of the greenery, to the cows and sheep a treat!
The pasture, the meadow, with grass so sweet.

So significant, so celebrated, the castles so old,
With each a story celebrated, with each a story told.
Enchanting, yet astounding, the mysteries these castles hold,
A glass of Scottish whiskey and let it all unfold.
How dreamy, how mysterious is the beautiful Scottish land?
Amazingly beautiful, simply Scotland.

70.

Dropped Me to School

In the haze of the morning mirror,
When the car windows were still white;
We rushed against the foggy wind, missing the street red light.
He drove as fast as a sports car, though it wasn't one,
May have been frantic for else but for us was strangely fun!
Racing away with my first man, the way we were used to,
Down the broad roads in the morning, that he would drive through.

Though it was a short journey, he made it a shorter while,
When we would reach, he'd open my door and give me a smile.
He wouldn't kneel down for any, being a man of charm and grace,
Yet I always made him kneel down, kneel down to tie my shoe lace.
And then he'd escort me to the gate, wasn't my hero cool?
The days my father dropped me, dropped me to school.

71.

Young Enough to Be a Teen

When the flaps of our bags would bother us and
we would drag ourselves under the sun,
And the sports teacher would simply say,
"Enjoy, these are the days of fun!"
When we would make excuses, yet the teacher wouldn't believe us,
We would tease each other with truth and dare...
spinning the bottle in the bus.

When we would brag about our crushes, we would laugh and boast,
Get ready just for that, that much awaited Instagram post.

We would try to catch the butterflies that flew above our head,
And try to perform the experiments from the science books we read.
When we would chat in the library instead of reading books,
The librarian would lower her specs and give us the sternest looks!

When we girls would say we want the finest of jewels,
The boys would say they want the finest car,
I now think about it and wonder,
Maybe we were wishing upon the wrong star.
I now too think about it and wonder how mischievous,
Rebellious youth we had been,
When we were just young enough, young enough to be a teen.

SCHOOL BUS

72.

Into the Hammock

As I lay on, my body feels light
but my mind becomes lighter it seems,
All the worry seems to fly away,
as the mind starts to switch to sweet dreams.
I stretch my knees and I let down my hair, let them touch the land,
As I yawn and pull my shoulders, let the flowers fall into my hand.

I look at the sky and think about the things,
think about things I truly admire,
As I listen to the leaves falling from the branches
and the squirrel moving higher.
I get a shade from the glowing, the warm glowing sun,
To others it may be boring but to me it was fun!

For I don't feed any effort, the wind does it for me,
It gives a few moments to relax, a ride, a pleasure for free.
Though laying on it was another film, it pushed away the stress,
For nothing else could make me heal, it was sure priceless.
It gave a press to my tired back, a rest to my tired feet,
For I waited all seasons long, only it comes use in the heat.
All rest starts to grow upon me, as into the cloth I duck,
When I sit and lay into, into the hammock.

Oops! I forgot to tell you.

73.

Forget Remembrance

The world is so full yet an empty place,
The reasoning is given thus,
For we don't choose memories but memories choose us.
What we may want to remember, might flow down the memory lane,
But they may choose to stay, the scars of suffering and pain.

We may not want to miss out on our dreams;
we'll forget their tales we fear,
But when we try to remember them, they oddly disappear!

Sometimes a name is stuck in our mind, but the face remains a blur,
I remember the name very well,
just forgot to remember which one is her.
Or sometimes a face is stuck in our mind,
but we don't know what to call.
Oh, is it a unique name or one cherished by all?

We ought to forget, we ought to remember, and our mind understands,
What we want to forget or want to remember, doesn't lie in our hands.
We may forget something we weren't supposed to,
Yet would lurk in our mind a small thing,
It happens to be funny sometimes, the act of remembering.
We shouldn't pressure ourselves, give up the idea of being tense,
And that is why I shall recommend, recommend to forget remembrance.

74.

Little Pleasures the Heart Needs

Twirling around in a long skirt, blowing away the dandelion seeds,
Thinking about the little pleasures, the little pleasures the heart needs.
The heart sometimes needs the pleasure,
Pleasure of a child having ice cream;
It many a times too needs the pleasure to look at the sky and dream.

It needs the pleasure to feel a little childhood,
And pay a visit to Disneyland,
Or the pleasure of getting a star or a little tattoo on the hand.
The heart only wants little pleasure, little pleasures from little deeds.
Thinking about the little pleasures, the little pleasures the heart needs.

75.

When Father Brought A New Toy

When father brought home a new toy,
He filled my little heart with joy.
I may have been little but not a little naive,
For I waited for him to return; return from work at five.

When in the morning, to office he would go,
Bring me a new toy, I'd let him know.
Often, he'd bring me little mirrors and makeup,
or sometimes even a teddy,
But to say no to me or to my demands father seldom was ready.

As when I wanted the big play house, he went to bring it from afar,
He may have wanted to buy himself one,
But first brought me a tiny sports car!
Now when I'm older I realise when father brought home a new toy,
He filled my little heart with memories, memories filled with joy.

SUMMER
CAMP

76.

Summer Camp

The little girls busy packing their bags, as each year they must,
Their mother's ready to drop them to camp, for they loved it as just.
To leave mischief at home this time, their mothers were imploring,
But the girls were all about having fun and hence went on ignoring.

As soon as they reached the camp, they settled into cute dorms,
The camp leaders then requested the girls to kindly follow the norms.
The girls acquired brilliance in their subjects, for their virtuous ranks,
But the girls acquired brilliance in mischief too,
for their well-played pranks.

They swam in the lake at sunset, mastering archery in the day,
Brunching along the pink dahlia in the torrid mist of May.
They picked up the wild mushrooms in their tiny baskets,
as well as fresh strawberries,
They washed the goodies while indulging in chatter,
under the shade of the trees.

At night, they lay on the grass and adored the stars shining,
Remembering how during the day they all tried zip lining,
Patted the white pony for a ride upon his back,
giving him yummy carrots to feed.
Collecting rocks of different shapes and sizes or cycling with full speed.

But when the camp was to be left, they carried the rocks,
the soil home in their backpack,
Already looking forward to the next summer camp,
when they will all come back.

77.

Spring Fair

It only comes up in the month of spring, a heavily crowded affair,
For each year, they deeply await, the mist of the spring fair.
Watching handmade puppet shows and not television cartoons,
The man with a bunch of handy rainbows, the joyous balloons.

Hearing the flute, the only music to hear,
The shops of the glass bangles, one that the girls line up near.
Little children flock by the sellers of sweetmeat,
While some give into the craving of popsicles in the spring heat.
While some still want to give the cool of the spring a turn,
By relishing the fried delights in return.

They plan to go after school, with their friends as a pair,
For each year they deeply await, the mist of the spring fair.

weet
h Shop

78.

Firework Festival

At the euphoric festival of fireworks and blinding illumination,
Not a seat to be freed in a while as gay crowds line up at the station.
All of them waiting to reach home, to reunite with their families,
Youth flying to meet their parents, all the way from overseas.

Little children blowing bubbles on their grandfather's backs,
Carrying little pouches with them to fill with money and snacks.
Relatives visiting from far away, to celebrate the festival of light,
to the euphoric festival of fireworks only for one night.

A hot pot for all, with a yummy barbeque,
Catching the fish from a little pond with a firework view.
Boys with a spirit of competition, lined up at the games station,
At the euphoric festival of fireworks and blinding illumination.

79.

Long Time Home

Newspapers from few months ago now
look like pages from history books,
Oh, it has been so long! I've forgotten how the world looks.
It has been so many days, I haven't been kissed,
kissed by the warmth of the sun
Oh, how I miss indulging a sunrise on my usual morning run.

Now I may recall the sweet chirping of birds, echoing in the clear blue skies,
Sad, I don't remember what they sound like, can only imagine through my eyes.
Aaah! What a delight! The fresh, cool wind blowing under the shade of trees,
But no one steps out anymore, even for their groceries.

I do remember my friend's faces, grateful for video calls,
Though I miss the time, I used to meet them in those gatherings in huge halls.
When mother would say you are grounded, that feeling was the worst,
Now I feel that pain has returned once more, once more to quench its thirst.

A fridge magnet from a city in another land, now looks like an ancient souvenir,
For seeing cars and pedestrians on the road, now has become pretty rare.
Even in the rain we took our umbrellas, nothing stopped us ever.
But now it just feels like it's been raining, it's been raining forever.

I've forgotten how the moon followed my car
and the way the stars speak,
It makes me sad that I can't even remember how the sun
and the clouds played hide and seek.
Newspapers from few months ago now, look like pages from history books.
Oh, it has been so long! I've forgotten how the world looks.

05
CHAPTER

Romance

80.

When I Speak of You

You can't see the milky way in mine, rather my eyes form a galaxy new,
And all the stars in that galaxy light up, light up when I speak of you.
Those eyes that close to the calming moon and
open to the sun that would burn,
But the moon or the sun don't seem to be
the sight for which these eyes yearn.

You can't see the love in my eyes, for the heart is where the love grew,
For even my heartbeats make a symphony,
symphony when I speak of you.
My heart seems to sing a song, a song which I never knew,
But a song that sounds like one you played, when I spoke of you.

All my sadness melts away as if I was never sad,
As if happiness was the only, was the only emotion I ever had.
As if a bird I became and into a book of fairytales I flew,
As if reality becomes my fairytale when I speak of you.

All my worry starts to wither, all my pain starts to shrink,
When I think about your smile, when I imagine the way you wink.
They seem to be on the verge, on the verge of coming true,
All my dreams, all my hopes all of them, when I speak of you.
The beauty of the moon was never doubted by me,
But one day it would be who knew,
For even the moon becomes jealous, jealous when I speak of you.

81.

Pretty Woman at the Patisserie

Each day on the way to my college, I'd stop at that pretty little patisserie,
For there a much prettier, young woman
would be waiting eagerly for me.
She knew my order of a dark espresso
and a pain au chocolate heated well,
She always kept it ready for me, never did I have to explain or tell.

Though she knew what I liked, what I wanted,
she never kept her change ready,
As an excuse to look for the change,
she'd try to spend more time with me.

I remember her sweet little dimples and her pink lipstick smile,
For she never stopped smiling for me, each smile lasting a long while.
Her neck used to adorn a golden necklace hanging
down to a deep buttoned satin shirt,
Her feet adored simple black heels moving up
to a washed off checkered skirt.
Her eyes adored a perfect winged eyeliner
which was always present without a fail,
Yet her brunette hair preferred to be, to be held by a messy fishtail.

She looked like another pretty girl of my age
but her thoughts sounded much young,
Oh, I remember some jingle from a fairy tale

that she often sung.
One day when I happened to go there as usual,
I learnt that the family had left the town,
The patisserie on the way to my college
was left alone and shut down.

82.

Hop Upon the Destiny Train

Hop upon the destiny train in the hope
that it will make us meet again.
Destiny is what brought us together yet it is what drove us away,
Spent without a thought of you, in my world not a day.

Your voice sonorous like metal, left ringing in my ear,
I feel your reflection touches me,
but when I open my eyes you disappear.
When I feel the drops pinching my skin,
I get soaked in the memories that rain,
Not a few questions left unanswered,
that keep me away from breathing sane.

A heart of glass can't be tamed, I tried with a mind of stone,
For it may have learnt to live, but hasn't forgotten to love alone.
Time to time back again, your love made up my thought,
How to live, how to not care, is what your love had taught.

When life was like a sinking ship and away, I wanted to run,
You made me feel to think that way, I wasn't the only one.
You taught me what I wouldn't learn, yet taught me to leave this way,
Yet I believe the force of love tries to bring us closer each day.

And that is why I tell you, to hop upon the destiny train,
In the hope that it will make us meet again.

83.

The Distance Between Us

Distance may be ill at ease for some, but to me it is not so,
For not bothered I am by the distance between us,
go as far as you want to go.

Feel free to become a bird and fly,
For I don't torment the distance, to you why would I lie?

The distance between us isn't tormented by me
but it is what I admire so purely true;
For if it weren't for the distance,
I wouldn't have had a reason to come closer to you.

Welcome

84.

The Strangers That We Were

My eyes peeked through a little gap, they found in the markets of thunder,
Why was it so enticing, they lay on my heart really does wonder?
A veil of shyness yet a smile of mischief,
it seemed what may have been,
But something enticing much, my eyes wouldn't have seen.

I could feel her walking ahead with every step I took,
I could savour her beauty,
I could savour her charm even without savouring a look!

I could hear her laughter which sounded
rather like sweetness dropping from the waterfall,
The sweetness in the reply of her voice as if someone did call.

My eyes could only be seen to be locked with her eyes.
Could only see them through the gap in the market shelves, otherwise.
Yet in the hustle of the moving markets,
I could tell from many which one was she,
For the tinkling of her anklets sounded still as joyful to me.

And then to take a step ahead, she smiled at me as I smiled at her,
And from that moment on we went to being,
went to being the strangers we were.

85.

Strangers on the Radio

Each day I listen to his voice on the radio,
of the silky stranger I hardly know.
Isn't he the reason I may drive at night,
Only to listen to his voice, when none is in sight,

When he takes the names of the callers at nine,
My heart seems to hear what may sound like mine.
When I am on the road and I feel alone,
I turn on the radio again to feel like home.

My heart calls out to the stranger I hear on the radio each day,
Hey stranger, listen to what this caller has to say.

Radio
FM
MW
SW
LW

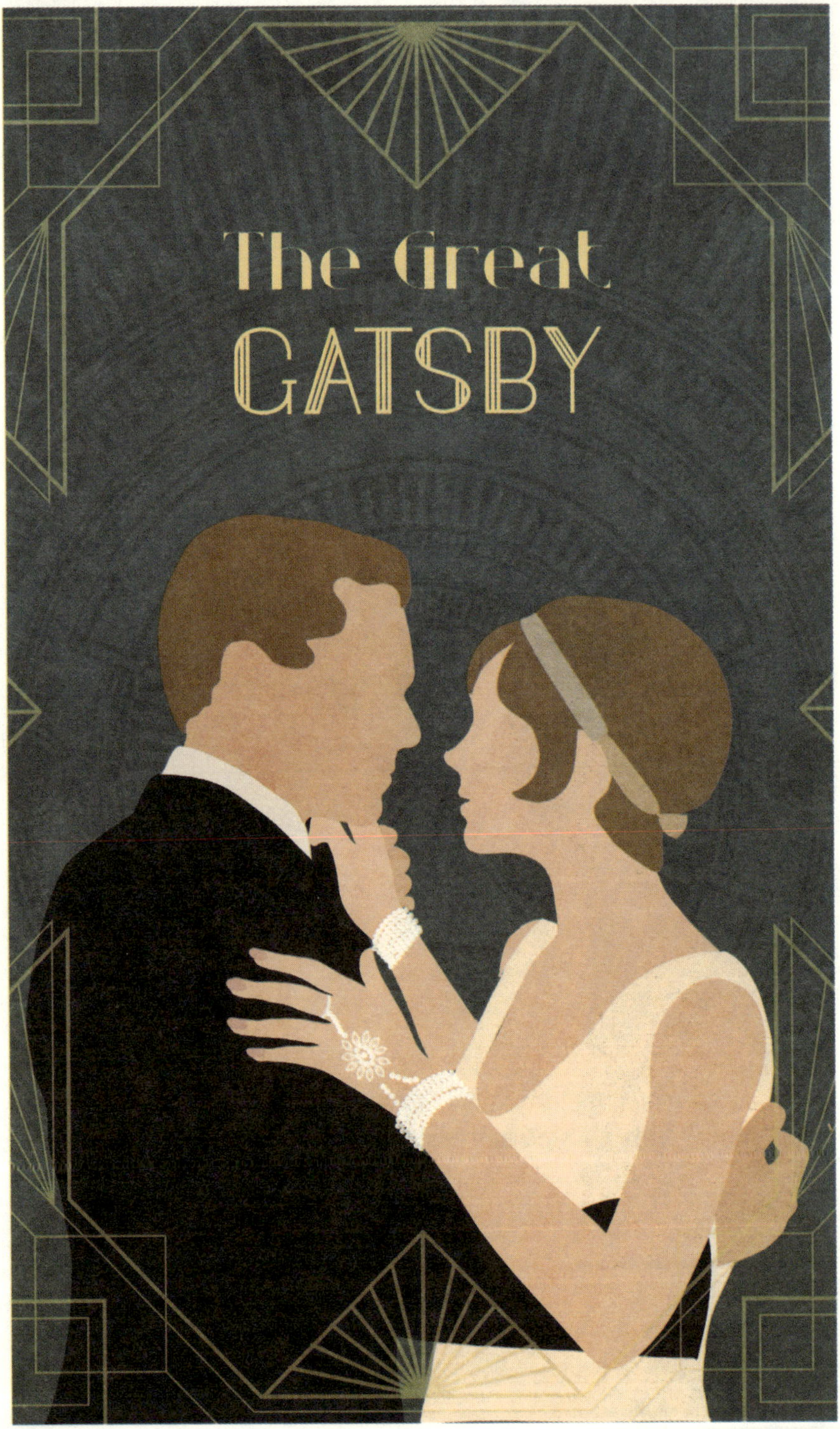
The Great
GATSBY

86.

After *The Great Gatsby*

They see life as a chain of events,
I see life as one big event to be in,
There is someone like me they wonder, all want to be him.
My life goes upwards since it has been from the start,
For I may hold the world in my palms yet hold an empty heart.

Only if I ever achieve the one across the green light,
Those parties I threw, hoping she'd wander in one night.
For the world can't fill my empty heart,
there is nothing to celebrate,
Yet I try to mould the pieces, the pieces of my broken fate.

Those parties charm several, for my palace has nothing to hide,
But who knows the one celebrating, is the one empty inside?
Some things are certain for you if you have wealth and will,
I had both, yet remained my heart empty still.

The day my love wanders in,
only then will be the day I truly Celebrate,
A man who wouldn't complete his story,
I wonder why they call great.
The day my celebration won't go to fail,
my love will come back to me,
Only then would I be known as the great Gatsby.

87.

Coming Back to the Shore

The ocean with a broken heart, for love it does lack,
To meet the shore, to love the shore, it keeps coming back.
The shore too seems to love the ocean, but doesn't seem to stay,
For it belongs to another world, nurtured miles away.

The ocean belongs to the world beneath, while the shore belongs to us,
The ocean and shore can't be together, the reason thus.
The ocean wants to stay with the shore, but it won't stay for long,
The shore too wants to be immersed, but would be rather wrong.

Tragic it is, how god framed the lovers' destiny,
The ocean and the shore love each other, but together can't ever be.
The ocean meets its lover, only for a while,
and keeps coming back for more,
That is why the ocean keeps coming back,
coming back to the shore.

88.

Memories I Hold, Memories I Held

The heart keeps longing for the moments long gone,
The moments we once spent together are now memories that I adorn.
Captured they are in my heart, not in a diary or a portal,
Those priceless memories that are immortal.

Whenever I walk through the woods, I feel you walking by my side,
Whenever I walk through the snow, I see myself in your jacket to hide.
Whenever I walk by the pond, I see a reflection of us dance,
Whenever I feel one upon me, I hope it is your glance.

Never told none what I thought, what I felt,
The memories I hold, the memories I held.

89.

Wasn't I Meant To Fall?

A day fine at work, down at the lobby but up in the sky,
Assembling the vases kept in the upper shelves,
held up by a ladder high.

A heavy bounce, a jerk occurred! Self, could I convince?
But when opened the eyes, unlikely revealed a charming prince.
The prince it was so sweet and charming,
yet silly enough to hit the ladder tall,
The prince so silly yet so charming, wasn't I meant to fall?

90.

Lovers of Vintage

The beauty of the silent woods, the lovers of vintage,
Where we have a little home, rather a cute cottage.
We sit by with our tea cups, waiting for it to snow,
We hide in our cute cottage, which no one else does know.

From one of the 1900's movies, in a little cottage in dark woods we stay,
From the movement of the city lights, just the two of us are away.
Where there is no other sound except our heartbeats through the doors,
Or could they be those footsteps, we locked on the wooden floors.
Hence, I called it, the lovers of vintage,
Where we have a little home, rather a cute cottage.

91.

Lover of the Moon

Gorgeous as much, seemingly from the figment of imagination,
But real it is thus truly a gem to a poet's reputation.
The gorgeous bud of nature, the mystical chukar,
For it is in love with the shining beauty, galaxy's biggest star.

It fell in love at first sight, the way that gaze lay upon,
The love so true and pure it seems, for it gazes from night to dawn.
Chukar loves the moon for it brings beauty to the galaxy black,
But no matter how much it would, the moon doesn’t seem to love back.

The love of the moon is hence, what would complete the chukar,
But could the moon ever love? Or only shine from afar?

92.

You And I

You see me as the winter wind, I see you as the summer breeze,
You and I are alike it seems yet stars of different galaxies.
Many there are songs about love, many that are sad but true,
But every song I hear about love,
sounds like a song about me and you,

You see me as a quiet lake, I see you as a vigorous waterfall,
You see me as the silent spirit, I see you as one who speaks to all.
Many there are romances in life, many loves that come and go,
For sometimes the mind has to take decisions that the heart
doesn't even wish to know.

The mind always seems to knit the truth, truths the heart
wouldn't ever savour,
Sometimes I too wish the mind spoke, spoke in the heart's favour.

You see me as one who remains attached to the memories, I see you
as one who lets them release,
You and I are alike it seems, yet stars of different galaxies.

06

CHAPTER

Feminist

93.

To the Friend I Lost

Sometimes the heart takes too long to accept,
accept what the mind already knows,
For when I look across the street, the light outside your house still glows.
I happen to dial your phone again or keep knocking at your door,
But suddenly, I realise there is no one to answer anymore.

Whenever I head to work, I look at your empty desk and wait,
But never did I lose hope, for I knew my friend always arrived late.

As I look at your half-burnt cigarettes there, I smoke them with my lighter,
Wrappers of your favourite chocolate underneath,
crumbles of pie in the keys of your typewriter.

I see your favourite novel kept with coffee
stained pages and a blue bookmark,
And I see your specs and a mini lamp,
for I knew you liked to read in the dark.
As I look into your novel, I feel my sinking heart,
I flip to page number 172; it was your favourite part.

As I peek into your drawer,
I happen to find the yearbook from school and our childhood,
I remember when we called each other names,
and you chased me around the neighbourhood.

I also see the keys to your first love, the keys to your first bike,
Along with a dusty picture of Julia from high school,
the one we both used to like.
In a time of another two months, I knew to visit New York you wished
I'd brought the tickets to surprise you,
but you left your dream unfinished.

For I take my hand to wipe my tear, on your chair,
your desk I sat, feel that French fragrance, I feel that perfume,
I knew you used to wear that.
I then go sit at my own desk but my heart
waits for you each day and goes,
For sometimes the heart takes too long to accept,
accept what the mind already knows.

94.

Soil of My Country

The blood that runs in my veins, a part of my identity,
The soil which my feet first lay upon, the soil of my country.
It is a soil that never has to take but only has to give,
It gives birth to a young soul; it gives us a life to live.

It gives us a name, it gives us one love, it gives us pride for eternity,
It becomes from where we feed ourselves,
it gives us more than we can see.
It gives us sweat, it gives us work, it gives us hope like the sun,
The soil that we live on, the soil that we work on,
it shall really be the one.

It becomes a nurturing mother to us, it gives us health and care,
It gives us a wholesome culture; it gives us opportunities to fare.
We shall be proud of who we are and what we are blessed to be,
Love and nurture the soil, the soil of my country.

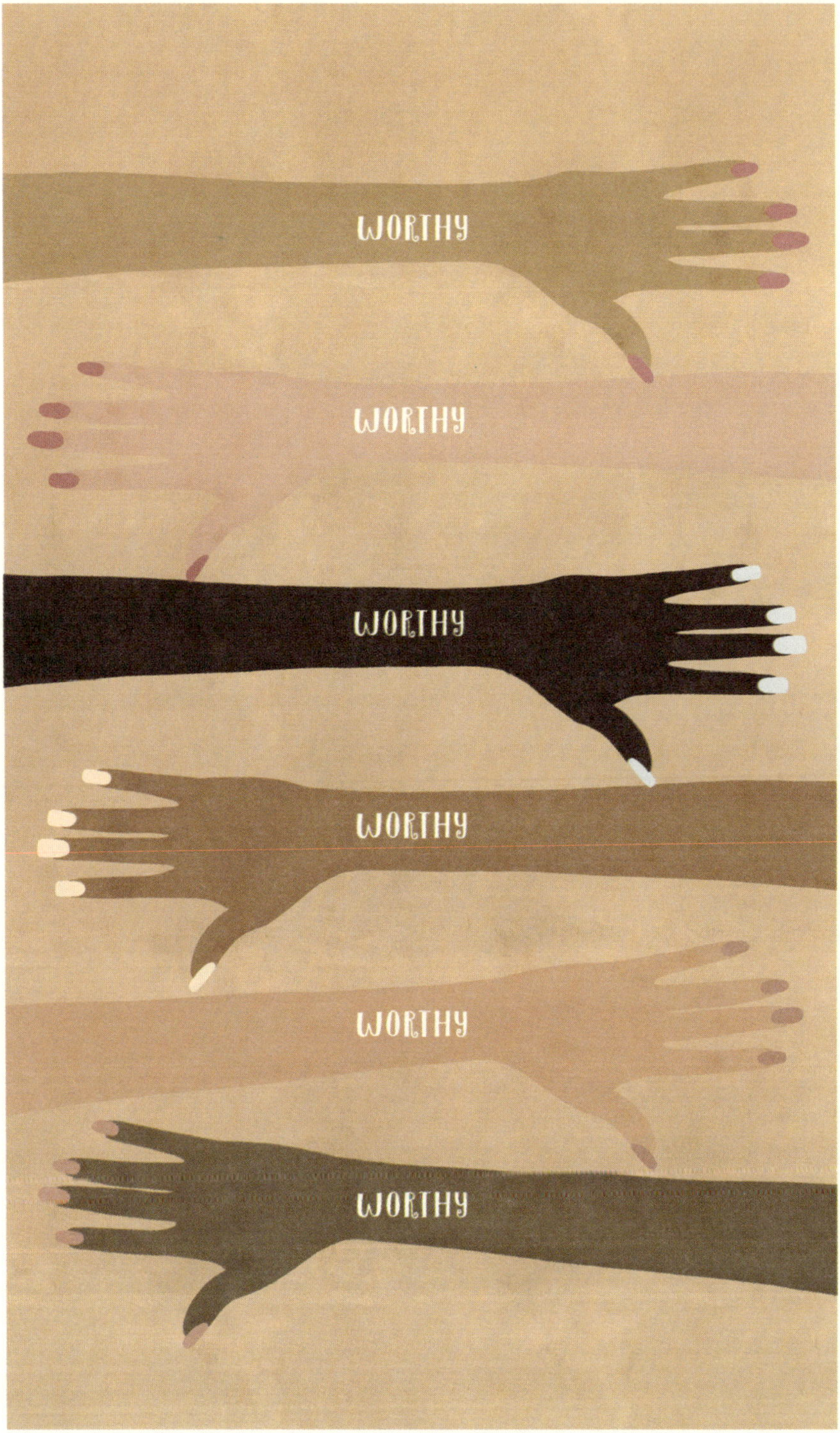
WORTHY
WORTHY
WORTHY
WORTHY
WORTHY
WORTHY

95.

In the Rage of Discrimination

Like a bird in migration, left the country in the rage of discrimination,
We were sought in order of the color of our skin,
The black ones, the losers, the white ones for the win.

All the provinces seemed to be ruled by the whites,
The black ones weren't even allowed their rights,
The white ones were wealthy and fine,
The black ones weren't even treated with a dime.

All the buses and schools under the white rules had no blacks allowed,
As they thought they would become polluted with the black crowd.
Now why I left my country? If you want to ask me,
Wasn't what I wanted but in the rage of discrimination.

EMBRACE ALL COLORS

96.

Golden Gore

The lives that were lost to shield us, weren't lives that lost but won,
The golden gore in the soil of the border, capturing the ardour of a gun.
For peerless vigour, selfless spirit in the battlefield
their souls attain liberation,
Devoted to the country till their very last breath,
true heroes of the nation.

Fearless men that fought for the country with an armour blood stained,
The war only grew tougher, but their courage remained.
Their bravery, their courage, such words would always fall short upon,
The lives that were lost to shield us weren't lives that lost but won.

97.

Magic in Her Hands

The power of her love, the power of her strength none can steal,
The wound she touches, the wound she fills is meant to heal.
Known to all, yet none understands,
She is not just a woman for there is magic in her hands.

She carves her body to give someone else one,
could there be a greater sacrifice?
Always keeps a smile on her face, even if pain is held in her eyes.

Her life isn't hers for she gives others a life,
More than just a woman, a sister, a mother, a wife.
She may have dreams,
she may have goals, but would never have the courage to confess,
For she knows her life is dedicated to fulfil the dreams of someone else.

Her sacrifice, her story known to all yet none understands,
She is not just a woman for there is magic in her hands.

07
CHAPTER
Me

98.

Only One

When the spotlight would fall upon me, peer through my reflection,
With the stage I stood on, would I feel a unique connection?

Several to capture me in their vision, several to judge and scorn,
Several to boost my confidence, several to admire and adorn.

Several sharing the stage with me, yet sharing the stage none,
For when I step on the stage, I feel I am the only one.

99.

What Is Poetry?

Poetry is addiction, sometimes reality, sometimes fiction,
Sometimes we think when we write, sometimes we don't.
Sometimes they have a happy ending, sometimes they won't.

Poetry is a beautiful form of expression,
Sometimes a secret, sometimes a confession.
Poetry is a rhyming notion,
Sometimes a feeling or a story in motion.
Poetry is an artistic delusion,
Sometimes classic, sometimes fusion.

And if you take a look from a poet's point of view,
Love in the air, romance in the rain,
It will all seem to come true.

100.

The Betty Who Wrote

The strings of passion loosening
themselves, becoming intangible so...
melting like burning candle wax
Plunged in rose ink, beside the fireplace...
the feather composing a fax.

Immersed to amazement there was a Betty young,
Allied to responses and onto responsibilities she clung.
Her mind naive and little yet a huge palace place,
For hidden somewhere in that palace, pleasured charm and grace.

Passion burning into the room yet loosely like the candle's wax,
I could read her little naive mind yet never what composed the fax.

101.

O Grandmother, Complete the Story

Each night before I went to sleep, a ritual we had before bedtime,
A story I liked we read for the night, for I wasn't too fond of the rhyme.

But in between the story, her head would lower down,
and on my neck slowly drop,
And I would yell,'Grandmother, continue! Why did the story stop?'
I'd take the book dropping from her hand
but just looking at the big words, I'd feel sick,
Oh, I wish to wake up grandmother, wake her up with a magical stick.

The part where the princess ran after the golden deer
into the deep dark forest,
That is the part she always falls asleep on,
Oh, when will I get to hear the rest?

Grandmother if we are stuck on one story,
when will we get to read more?
It makes me feel so bored, when I listen to her growing snore.
Each time I would realise it when
her voice would become slower and break,
I'd realise again like yesterday, I am the only one awake.

The story is an interesting one, the ending I want to know,
But if she wouldn't fall asleep,

we would have finished the book long ago.
Though the story is to put me to sleep, it makes her fall asleep,
So, I take the book from her hand and in my cupboard I go and keep.

Each night I'd make her begin from the start,
yet interesting much it hasn't been,
For there was never a time, she wouldn't fall asleep in between.

The magic of a grandmother telling stories is so
fun for a child when it continues with a flow,
And that is why I tell her to complete, complete the story
before older I grow.

Listening to our elders but only for their stories,
it is really the joy of childhood to last,
Listening to the stories we wouldn't realise,
how years went by so fast.
I tell my grandmother to complete her tale,
of the princess and her glory,
O grandmother, complete it please,
O grandmother, complete the story.

Acknowledgments

Hello everyone!

Poetry and rhyming words have always fascinated me. When I read poems by famous authors, I am intrigued by the choice of words and their profound wisdom. Sheer magic!

This romance of words has inspired me. I decided to write poetry on my own and here I am sharing my thoughts with you all. I'm super grateful to achieve this dream, my very own first book, my words, my gift to myself.

Heartfelt thanks to Mrs. Anshu Khanna for being a pillar of support and for her guidance in making this dream possible.

Thank you Mr. Ajay Mago for believing in my dreams and holding my hand through this journey. Thank you, my adorable family, for your incredible love and support. Thank you Chakrika for editing my book. Thank you Shruti Ahuja for making the beautiful illustrations that perfectly accompany my poems.